FOUNDAT

AN ADMONITION CONCERNING RELICS

JOHN CALVIN

Printed and Published by
John Metcalfe Publishing Trust
Church Road, Tylers Green
Penn, Buckinghamshire

—

Distributed by Trust Representatives
and Agents world-wide

In the Far East

Bethany, Orchard Point P.O. Box 0373
Singapore 9123

—

© John Metcalfe Publishing Trust 1995
All Rights Reserved

—

First Published May 1995

—

ISBN 1 870039 63 7

—

Price 25p

—

AN ADMONITION CONCERNING RELICS

AUGUSTINE, in his work, entitled, 'On the Labour of Monks', complaining of certain itinerant impostors, who, as early as his day, plied a vile and sordid traffic, by carrying the relics of martyrs about from place to place, adds, 'If, indeed, they are relics of martyrs.' By this expression, he intimates the prevalence, even in his day, of abuses and impostures, by which the ignorant populace were cheated into the belief, that bones gathered here and there were those of saints.

While the origin of the imposture is thus ancient, there cannot be a doubt that in the long period which has since elapsed, it has exceedingly increased, considering, especially, that the world has since been strangely corrupted, and has never ceased to become worse, till it has reached the extreme wherein we now behold it.

But the first abuse, and, as it were, beginning of the evil, was, that when Christ ought to have been sought in his word, sacraments, and spiritual influences, the world, after its wont, clung to his garments, vests, and swaddling-clothes; and thus overlooking the principal matter, followed only its accessory.

The same course was pursued in regard to apostles, martyrs, and other saints. For when the duty was to meditate diligently on their lives, and engage in imitating them, men made it their whole study to contemplate and lay up, as it were in a treasury, their bones, shirts, girdles, caps, and similar trifles.

Let us begin then with Christ. As his natural body could not be possessed, (though some have found an easy way of fabricating miraculous bodies for him, in whatever numbers, and with whatever frequency they please,) instead of it they have collected six hundred frivolities to compensate for its absence. They have not even allowed the body of Christ to escape entirely, but have managed to retain a portion.

Next comes the blood, about which there have been great disputes. For very many have maintained, that no blood of Christ exists, except what is miraculous. And yet his natural blood is exhibited in more than a hundred places; in some of them, as at Rochelle in Aunis, in a few drops which Nicodemus is said to have received in his handkerchief; in others, in full phials, as at Mantua. At Billom in Auvergne, it is shown in a crystal vase, in the form of a liquid, while, at a village in the same neighbourhood, and in other places, it is coagulated. Elsewhere, as in the church of Eustathius at Rome, it is poured from full goblets.

Nor was it enough to have pure blood; they must needs also have it mingled with water, as it flowed from our Saviour's side when it was pierced on the cross. This ware is found at Rome in the church of Joannes Lateranensis. I leave every man to judge what certainty can be had on such a subject, and whether it be not a manifest falsehood to say that the blood of Christ has been found seven or eight hundred years after his death, and in such quantities as to be diffused over the whole world, and this without any mention of it whatever in the ancient church.

Let us now come to relics of the last supper, which Christ celebrated with the apostles. The table is at Rome, in the church of Joannes Lateranensis, some of the bread in that of St. Salvator in Spain, while the knife with which the Paschal Lamb was cut up is at Treves.

Be it observed, Christ celebrated the supper in a hired room, and, of course, on quitting it, left the table behind. Nor do we read that it was carried off by the apostles. Some years after, as we have said, Jerusalem was destroyed. What semblance of probability is there, that that table was found out seven or eight hundred years after? Besides, tables were at that time quite different in shape from those now in use. For at meals, the custom was not to sit, but to recline; this is clearly shown in the gospel. There is here, therefore, a manifest falsehood.

What more? At the church of Mary Insulane, near Lyons, is shown the cup which contained the sacrament of his blood which he gave to the apostles to drink. It is also to be seen in the Vivarais in a certain monastery of Augustins. Which are we to believe?

But the case is still worse with the dish in which the Paschal Lamb was placed. For it is at Rome, and at Genoa, and at Arles. Perhaps the custom of that time was different from ours. For as in the present day, a variety of meats are put into one dish; so there must then have been various dishes for one meat, if credit is to be given to these holy relics. Can falsehood be more clearly proved?

The same thing occurs in the case of the linen towel with which our Saviour wiped the feet of the apostles, after he had washed them. There is one at Rome, in the church of Joannes Lateranensis, and another at Acqs in Germany, in the church of Cornelius, with the mark of Judas' foot upon it; one or other of these must be spurious.

What, then, shall our judgment be? Let us leave them to debate the matter among themselves, until one shall have made out something like a case. Meanwhile, let us hold it a mere imposition to attempt to persuade men that a towel, which our Saviour left in the house in which he celebrated the supper, took its flight to Italy or Germany, five or six hundred years after the destruction of Jerusalem.

The cross which Helena, the mother of the Emperor Constantine, found is said to be still at Jerusalem. And no one calls this in question, though it is plainly inconsistent with ecclesiastical history, which relates that Helena sent part of it to the emperor her son, by whom it was placed on a pillar of porphyry at Constantinople; and that she inclosed the remainder in a silver chest, which she gave to the Bishop of Jerusalem for preservation. Therefore, we must either accuse the history of falsehood, or the things told of the true cross in the present day are utterly vain and frivolous.

Again, let us consider how many fragments of it are scattered up and down over the whole globe. A mere enumeration of those of which I have a catalogue would certainly fill a goodly volume. There is no town, however small, which has not some morsel of it, and this not only in the principal cathedral church of the district, but also in parish churches. There is no abbey so poor as not to have a specimen. In some places, larger fragments exist, as at Paris, in the Holy Chapel, at Poictiers, and at Rome, where a crucifix of tolerable size is said to have been entirely made out of it.

In fine, if all the pieces which could be found were collected into a heap, they would form a good ship-load, though the gospel testifies, that a single individual was able to carry it. What effrontery, then, thus to fill the whole world with fragments, which it would take more than three hundred men to carry? But they have fallen upon an explanation, and it is, that how much soever may be cut from it, it never grows less. But this device is too foolish and absurd for the superstitious themselves not easily to see through it.

I leave it to all men to consider what certainty can be had as to the genuineness of all the pieces of wood which are worshipped in all the different places as the true cross. Whence certain fragments were brought, and by what way and means, I omit to say; some affirming that they were brought to them by angels, others that they dropped from heaven. Those of Poictiers say, that the piece which they have was stolen by a maid-servant of Helena, and carried off, and that she having afterwards fled, brought it, in the course of her wanderings, into that district. They also add to the story that she was lame. Such are the illustrious grounds on which they stimulate the wretched populace to idolatry.

And not contented with imposing on the rude and ignorant, by displaying a piece of common wood as the wood of the cross, they have declared it every way worthy of adoration. The doctrine is altogether devilish, and Ambrose expressly condemns it as heathen superstition.

We must now consider the napkin, as to which they have still more openly betrayed their impudence and stupidity. For, besides the napkin of Veronica, which is exhibited at St. Peter's, and the robe which the Virgin Mary is said to have wrapped round our Saviour, and which is shown in the church of Joannes Lateranensis, and also in the Augustin monastery at Carcassone, they have also the napkin in which our Saviour's head was wrapped in the sepulchre. This is exhibited at the same place.

There are, at least, six cities more which boast of having this very napkin, as the one at Nice, which was brought from Cambray, also those at Acqs in Germany, at Maestricht, at Besancon, and also at Vindon in Limoges, also in a certain town in Lorraine, on the borders of Alsace; besides portions of it which are scattered up and down in different places, as at St. Salvator's in Spain, and in a monastery of Augustins in the Vivarais.

I say nothing of that complete napkin, which exists in a certain nunnery at Rome, as the Pope has expressly prohibited the exhibition of it. Must not men, I ask, have been exceedingly infatuated, to travel so far, at great expense, and with greater trouble, to see a bit of cloth, as to which not the least certainty could be had, or rather as to which they must, of necessity, have had their doubts?

For whosoever believes that this napkin exists in one particular place, brings a charge of falsehood against all the others which boast that they possess it. For instance, he who believes that the piece of cloth which was at Cambray is the genuine napkin, condemns those of Besancon, of Acqs, of Vindon, of Maestricht, and of Rome, as guilty of falsehood and of wickedness, inasmuch as they stimulate the people to idolatry, and impose upon them, by making them believe that a bit of common cloth is the linen which wrapped our Saviour's body in the tomb.

To proceed in order, we must now consider the case of John the Baptist, who, according to the account given in the gospel, that is, according to the truth of God, after being beheaded, was buried by his disciples. Theodoret relates that his sepulchre, which was at Sebastia, a town of Syria, was some time afterwards opened by the heathen, who burned the body, and scattered the ashes to the wind. It is true, indeed, Eusebius adds, that some inhabitants of Jerusalem came and secretly carried off a portion, which they removed to Antioch, and which Athanasius afterwards inclosed within a wall. Sozomen wrote that the head was conveyed to Constantinople by the Emperor Theodosius.

The testimony of ancient history, therefore, is, that the whole body was burned, with the exception of the head, and that all the bones and all the ashes were scattered, except a very small portion, which was carried off by some hermits of Jerusalem.

Now, let us see how much is said to be extant. The people of Amiens say that they have the front part of the head; and in the skull exhibited by them a wound appears, which they say Herodias inflicted with a knife. The inhabitants of Joannes Angelicus contradict them, and show the very same part. But the remainder of the head, viz., that reaching from the forehead back to the neck, was formerly in Rhodes, and is now, I think, in Malta; at least the Templars did pretend that it was restored to them by the Turks. The back of the head is at Nevers, and the brain at Novium Rantroviensis.

And yet, notwithstanding, part of the head is in the church of Joannes Moirienus. Then his jaws are at Besancon, in the church of John the Elder. Another part is at Paris, in the church of Joannes Lateranensis, and the tip of the ear is at Sanflor, in Auvergne, while the forehead and the hair is in St. Salvator's in Spain. At Noyon, also, is a certain portion, which is wont to be exhibited in great state. There is also a part, but I know not what, at Lucca.

Is all this true? Go to Rome, and you will hear that the whole head of John is in the monastery of Sylvester. Poets feign that in Spain there once lived a king, named Geryon, who had three heads. If our fabricators of relics could say the same thing of John the Baptist, it would be a great help to their lies. But since there is no room for such a fable, to what excuse will they resort?

I am unwilling to press them so far as to ask how his head was cut into such minute portions as to become capable of distribution in so many various places, or how they got it out of Constantinople. I only say that John must have been a monster, or that they are impudent impostors in exhibiting so many fragments of his head.

But this is not the worst. For the people of Sienna say that they have got his arm, an allegation contradicted, as we have already observed, by all ancient history. Nevertheless, the imposture is tolerated, nay even approved; for in the kingdom of Antichrist nothing is thought wicked which tends to increase the superstition of the people.

Besides, they have invented another fable, viz., that when his body was burned, the finger with which he pointed out Christ to his two disciples remained entire, and was not injured in the least. But this not only does not accord with ancient history, but may easily be confuted by it. For Eusebius and Theodoret relate that when the Gentiles seized the body it was all consumed to the very bones. Assuredly, had anything so miraculous happened with regard to the finger, they would not have omitted to mention it; for in other repects they are rather too fond of narrating such trifles.

But supposing the fact to be as alleged, let us see for a little where this finger is to be found. There is one at Besancon, in the church of John the Great, another at Tholouse, another at Lyons, another at Bourges, another at Florence, and another at the church of Fortuitus, near Mascon.

All I would do here is to ask my readers not to harden themselves against evidence so clear and certain—not to close their eyes in such bright light, and allow themselves to be led astray, as it were, in the dark. If there were jugglers, who could so impose on our eyesight as to make it appear that there were six fingers on one hand, we would yet guard cautiously against imposture, and try to detect it. Here, however, there is nothing that even looks like a clever trick.

Now let the apostles come forward in order. Their number, however, may beget confusion; and, therefore, the better course will be to take Paul and Peter by themselves, and afterwards proceed to the rest. Their bodies are at Rome, half at St. Peter's, and half at St. Paul's, Sylvester having, it is said, weighed them to make sure of an equal division. The heads of both are in the church of Joannes Lateranensis, though in the same church there is a tooth of Peter existing separately by itself.

Though these things are so, it does not prevent them from being in other places also, as at Poictiers, where they have Peter's cheek-bone and his beard. At Treves they have many bones belonging to both, and at Argenton, in Berri, they have Paul's shoulder. But the thing is endless. Wherever there are churches dedicated to them, they have their relics in abundance.

If it be asked, what kind of relics? let them call to mind what kind of a one the brain of St. Peter was which I formerly mentioned, and which stood on the high altar of this city. As it turned out to be a pumice stone, so, on inquiry, it will be found, that many of the bones which are attributed to these apostles are those either of horses or dogs.

Then come the things belonging to the bodies, as accessories. For instance, there is a shoe at St. Salvator's in Spain, but of what form and material I am unable to say. But the probability is, that it is an article of a similar description to the shoes which they have at Poictiers, and which are made of polished leather, ornamented with gold. See how splendidly they have adorned him after death, to compensate for the poverty in which he passed his life!

As the bishops of the present day, in representing pontifical majesty, are so splendidly clothed, it would seem to derogate from the dignity of the apostles, were not something of the same nature attributed to them. True! painters can draw pictures in what colours they please, decking them from top to toe in varied attire, and then give them the name of Peter and Paul, or any other name; but everybody knows the kind of clothing which they actually had in this world, and that it was no better than that which is usually worn by the poor.

They have also at Rome the episcopal chair in which Peter sat, together with the sacerdotal robe in which he used to say mass, as if bishops had at that time sat on thrones. Their business rather was to teach, comfort, and exhort in public and private, and make themselves ensamples to the flock; not to show themselves to the people to be adored by them, as the prelates of our day are wont to do.

With regard to the robe for mass, the custom of masking after the manner of players was not then introduced; for plays were not then acted in the church as they are now. Wherefore, in order to prove that Peter was dressed in a missal robe, they must first show that when he worshipped God he performed the part of a player like the popish priests. It was natural enough for them to give him a missal robe, as they had previously given him an altar; but there is no more plausibility in the one than in the other.

What kind of masses was then celebrated is well known; for the apostles in their time only celebrated the Lord's supper, and for this no altar was necessary. That kind of monstrosity called a mass was altogether unknown, and continued to be unknown for long after. Hence it is clear, that these men, in fabricating their relics, must have supposed they were never to meet with an opponent; so shamelessly and extravagantly have they dared to lie. And yet they are not agreed among themselves as to that altar. For the Romans say that they have it, while the people of Pisa also show it in their suburb which faces the sea.

But that they might lose no possible means of making profit, they have not forgotten the sword with which the ear of Malchus was cut off, as if it were some fair ornament worthy of being preserved as a relic. I have omitted to mention the staff which is shown at Paris in the church of St. Stephen á Pierre, and which is in as high repute as the altar and missal robe, and just for as good a reason. As to the staff, there is somewhat more plausibility in it, as it is not unlikely he may have used a staff in travelling; but then they throw everything into confusion, by not agreeing among themselves about it. For the inhabitants of Cologne, and likewise those of Treves, contend for the possession of it. While they accuse each other of falsehood, they furnish us with good grounds for not giving credit to either.

As to the chain with which Peter was bound I say nothing. It is shown at Rome in the church which bears its name. Nor do I say anything of the pillar on which he was beheaded, and which is shown in the church of St. Anastasius. I only leave my readers to reflect how that chain must have been procured for the purpose of being converted into relics, and also whether, at that time, it was customary for executions to take place upon pillars.

We will now consider the case of the other apostles jointly, and will dispose of it in a very few words. And first, we will mention where the whole bodies are, that by comparing them together, it may be seen what certainty can be had in reference to the things said of them. Everybody knows that the inhabitants of Tholouse think that they have got six of these bodies, viz., those of James the Greater, Andrew, James the Less, Philip, Simeon, and Jude. The body of Matthias is at Padua, that of Matthew, at Salerno, of Thomas, at Ortona, and of Bartholomew, at Naples, or somewhere in that district.

Now, let us attend to those who have had two or three bodies. For Andrew has another body at Melfi, Philip and James the Less have each another body at the church of the Holy Apostles, and Simeon and Jude, in like manner, at the church of St. Peter. Bartholomew has also another in the church dedicated to him at Rome. So here are six who have each two bodies, and also by way of a supernumerary, Bartholomew's skin is shown at Pisa.

Matthias, however, surpasses all the rest, for he has a second body at Rome, in the church of the Elder Mary, and a third one at Treves. Besides, he has another head, and another arm, existing separately by themselves. There are also fragments of Andrew existing at different places, and quite sufficient to make up half a body. For his head is at Rome, at the church of St. Peter, a shoulder in that of Grisgon, a rib in that of St. Eustathius, an arm in that of the Holy Spirit, and some other part in the church of St. Blaise. There is also a foot at Aix. Were all these joined together, and properly fitted, they would make up two quarters of the body.

But as Bartholomew left his skin at Pisa, so also he has left one of his heads at Treves, and some other member, I know not what. He has also a finger at Frene, while some other relics of them exist also at Rome, in the church of St. Barbara. Thus, there is not only no want, but a superfluity in his case.

The others are not so well supplied, yet each of them has somewhat to spare. For Philip has one foot at Rome, in the church of the Holy Apostles; also in the church of St. Barbara he has I know not what relics, besides these which he has at Treves. In these two last churches he has James for his companion; for James, in like manner, has a hand in the church of St. Peter, an arm in that of Grisgon, and another in that of the Holy Apostles.

Matthew and Thomas have been left poorer than the rest. For the former has only one body, together with a few bones at Treves, and an arm at Rome, in the church of St. Marcellus, and a head in that of St. Nicholas, unless there be some which have escaped me. This is very likely; for how can one avoid losing one's self in such a labyrinth?

The other things must be briefly dispatched; for otherwise we should never be able to get out of this forest. We shall merely mention a few of the alleged relics of saints who lived in the days of our Saviour, and then mention a few of those of the ancient martyrs and others. In this way my readers will be able to judge for themselves.

Anna, mother of the Virgin Mary, has one of her bodies at Apte in Provence, and another in the church of Mary Insulane at Lyons. Besides, she has one of her hands at Treves, another at Turin, and a third in a town of Thuringia, which takes its name from it. I say nothing of the fragments which exist in more than a hundred places. Among others, I remember having myself, long ago, kissed a portion of it at Ursicampus, a monastery in the vicinity of Noyon, where it is held in great reverence. Lastly, another of her arms is in St. Paul's at Rome. Here, if it be possible, let some certainty be shown.

But anyone may ask, how have these fabricators of relics omitted the many notable things connected with the old dispensation, since, without any regard to reason, they have heaped up all that ever came into their mind, and, as it were with a breath, called into existence whatever they pleased?

To this question I can give no other answer than that they did not think it worth their while, because they had no prospect of deriving much advantage from such relics; and yet they have not forgotten them entirely, for at Rome they gave out that they have the bones of Abraham, Isaac, and Jacob, in the church of Mary supra Minerva.

They also boast that in the church of Joannes Lateranensis they have the ark of the covenant and Aaron's rod within it. The same rod, however, is at Paris in the Holy Chapel, while some fragment of it also is in St. Salvator's in Spain. I omit the inhabitants of Bourdeaux, who maintain that the rod of St. Martial, which is exhibited in the church of Severinus, is the identical rod of Aaron.

It would seem that they had wished to perform a new miracle as in rivalship of God; for whereas he, by his power, turned the rod into a serpent, so they have now turned it into three rods. Very probably they have many other toys of the same description, but let it suffice merely to have mentioned this, in order to make it manifest that they have been as honest here as in other matters.

To draw to a conclusion, I beseech my readers, in the name of God, to give heed to the truth while it lies plainly before them, and recognize how divine providence has wonderfully provided, that those who thus wished to mislead the meanest of the people have been so blind that they never thought of using a cloak for their lies, but moving blindfolded, like the Midianites, have set about slaughtering one another.

As we see how they are still warring among themselves, and charging each other with falsehood, every man, who is not obstinately determined against the truth, though he may not yet clearly perceive that the worship of any relics, of whatever kind they be, whether genuine or spurious, is execrable idolatry, yet seeing how clear their falsehood is, will have no desire to kiss them any more, and whatever reverence they may have previously inspired, will cease to have any relish for them.

The best thing, indeed, would be, as I mentioned at the outset, if, among us who profess the name of Christ, this heathenish custom were abolished, whether they be relics of Christ or of the saints. Inasmuch as they do degenerate into idols, the pollution and defilement which they occasion ought not on any account to be tolerated in the church. This we have already demonstrated, both by argument and by the testimony of scripture.

Wherefore, if a complete reformation of this corrupt practice is desired, it will be necessary to begin at the very foundation, and abolish a practice which was at first instituted improperly, and against all reason. But if any one is not able at one step to make such an advance towards true understanding, let him at least proceed gradually. And, in the first place, let him open his eyes, and exercise his judgment upon any relics which may be presented to him. No one inclined to make the attempt will find it at all difficult; for among the many transparent lies, such as those to which I have already adverted, where will any relics be found whose genuineness amounts to anything like certainty?

The number of similar follies is indeed infinite, and a careful inspection would discover more than it is possible to enumerate. Let every one, then, be on his guard, and not allow himself to be led along like an irrational animal, and as if he were incapable of discerning any way or path by which he might be guided safely.

I recollect when I was a boy how they were wont to do with the images of our parish. When the feast of Stephen drew near, they adorned them all alike with garlands and necklaces, just decking the murderers who stoned Stephen in the same way as they decked Stephen himself. When the old women saw the murderers thus adorned, they imagined that they were Stephen's companions. Accordingly, every one was presented with his candle. Nay, the same honour was conferred on the devil who contended with Michael, and so on with the rest.

And so completely are they all mixed up and huddled together, that it is impossible to have the bones of any martyr without running the risk of worshipping the bones of some thief or robber, or, it may be, the bones of a dog, or a horse, or an ass. Nor can the Virgin Mary's ring, or comb, or girdle, be venerated without the risk of venerating some part of the dress of a strumpet. Let every one, therefore, who is inclined, guard against this risk. Henceforth no man will be able to excuse himself by pretending ignorance.

JOHN CALVIN
(1509-1564)

MINISTRY BY JOHN METCALFE

TAPE MINISTRY BY JOHN METCALFE
FROM ENGLAND AND THE FAR EAST
IS AVAILABLE.

In order to obtain this free recorded ministry, please send your blank cassette (C.90) and the cost of the return postage, including your name and address in block capitals, to the John Metcalfe Publishing Trust, Church Road, Tylers Green, Penn, Bucks, HP10 8LN. Tapelists are available on request.

Owing to the increased demand for the tape ministry, we are unable to supply more than two tapes per order, except in the case of meetings for the hearing of tapes, where a special arrangement can be made.

Book Order Form

Please send to the address below:-

	Price	Quantity
A Question for Pope John Paul II	£1.25	......
Of God or Man?	£1.45	......
Noah and the Flood	£1.90	......
Divine Footsteps	£0.95	......
The Red Heifer	£0.75	......
The Wells of Salvation	£1.50	......
The Book of Ruth (Hardback edition)	£4.95	......
Divine Meditations of William Huntington	£2.35	......
Present-Day Conversions of the New Testament Kind	£2.25	......
Saving Faith	£2.25	......
Deliverance from the Law	£1.90	......
The Beatitudes	£1.90	......
Colossians	£0.95	......
Philippians	£1.90	......
Matthew	£0.95	......
Philemon	£1.90	......

Psalms, Hymns & Spiritual Songs (Hardback edition)

The Psalms of the Old Testament	£2.50	......
Spiritual Songs from the Gospels	£2.50	......
The Hymns of the New Testament	£2.50	......

'Apostolic Foundation of the Christian Church' series

Foundations Uncovered	Vol.I	£0.75	......
The Birth of Jesus Christ	Vol.II	£0.95	......
The Messiah (Hardback)	Vol.III	£7.75	......
The Son of God and Seed of David (Hardback)	Vol.IV	£6.95	......
Christ Crucified (Hardback)	Vol.V	£6.95	......
Justification by Faith (Hardback)	Vol.VI	£7.50	......
The Church: What is it? (Hardback)	Vol.VII	£7.75	......

Name and Address (in block capitals)

. . . .

. . . .

. . . .

If money is sent with order please allow for postage. Please address to:- The John Metcalfe Publishing Trust, Church Road, Tylers Green, Penn, Bucks, HP10 8LN.

THE MINISTRY OF THE NEW TESTAMENT

The purpose of this substantial A4 gloss paper magazine is to provide spiritual and experimental ministry with sound doctrine which rightly and prophetically divides the Word of Truth.

Readers of our books will already know the high standards of our publications. They can be confident that these pages will maintain that quality, by giving access to enduring ministry from the past, much of which is derived from sources that are virtually unobtainable today, and publishing a living ministry from the present. Selected articles from the following writers have already been included:

ELI ASHDOWN · ABRAHAM BOOTH · JOHN BRADFORD
JOHN BUNYAN · JOHN BURGON · JOHN CALVIN · DONALD CARGILL
JOHN CENNICK · J.N. DARBY · GEORGE FOX · JOHN FOXE
WILLIAM GADSBY · JOHN GUTHRIE · WILLIAM GUTHRIE
GREY HAZLERIGG · WILLIAM HUNTINGTON · WILLIAM KELLY
JOHN KENNEDY · JOHN KERSHAW · HANSERD KNOLLYS
JAMES LEWIS · MARTIN LUTHER · ROBERT MURRAY MCCHEYNE
JOHN METCALFE · ALEXANDER—SANDY—PEDEN · J.C. PHILPOT
J.K. POPHAM · JAMES RENWICK · J.B. STONEY · HENRY TANNER
ARTHUR TRIGGS · JOHN VINALL · JOHN WARBURTON
JOHN WELWOOD · GEORGE WHITEFIELD · J.A. WYLIE

Price £1.75 *(postage included)*
Issued Spring, Summer, Autumn, Winter.

Magazine Order Form

Name and Address (in block capitals)

. . . .
. . . .
. . . .

Please send me .... current copy/copies of The Ministry of the New Testament.

Please send me .... year/s subscription.

I enclose a cheque/postal order for £ ....

(Price: including postage, U.K. £1.75; Overseas £1.90)
(One year's subscription: Including postage, U.K. £7.00; Overseas £7.60)

Cheques should be made payable to The John Metcalfe Publishing Trust, and for overseas subscribers should be in pounds sterling drawn on a London Bank.

10 or more copies to one address will qualify for a 10% discount

Back numbers from Spring 1986 available.

Please send to The John Metcalfe Publishing Trust, Church Road, Tylers Green, Penn, Buckinghamshire, HP10 8LN.

All Publications of the Trust are subsidised by the Publishers.

Tract Order Form

Please send to the address below:-

	Price	Quantity
Evangelical Tracts		
The Two Prayers of Elijah	£0.10	......
Wounded For Our Transgressions	£0.10	......
The Blood of Sprinkling	£0.10	......
The Grace of God That Brings Salvation	£0.10	......
The Name of Jesus	£0.10	......
The Death of the Righteous by A.M.S.	£0.10	......
The Ministry of the New Testament	£0.10	......
Repentance	£0.10	......
Legal Deceivers Exposed	£0.10	......
Unconditional Salvation	£0.10	......
Religious Merchandise	£0.10	......
Comfort	£0.10	......
Peace	£0.10	......
Eternal Life	£0.10	......
The Handwriting of Ordinances	£0.10	......
'Lord, Lord!'	£0.10	......

Name and Address (in block capitals)

. . . .

. . . .

. . . .

If money is sent with order please allow for postage. Please address to:- The John Metcalfe Publishing Trust, Church Road, Tylers Green, Penn, Bucks, HP10 8LN.

Tract Order Form

Please send to the address below:-

		Price	Quantity
'Tract for the Times' series			
The Gospel of God	No.1	£0.25	......
The Strait Gate	No.2	£0.25	......
Eternal Sonship and Taylor Brethren	No.3	£0.25	......
Marks of the New Testament Church	No.4	£0.25	......
The Charismatic Delusion	No.5	£0.25	......
Premillennialism exposed	No.6	£0.25	......
Justification and Peace	No.7	£0.25	......
Faith or presumption?	No.8	£0.25	......
The Elect undeceived	No.9	£0.25	......
Justifying Righteousness	No.10	£0.25	......
Righteousness Imputed	No.11	£0.25	......
The Great Deception	No.12	£0.25	......
A Famine in the Land	No.13	£0.25	......
Blood and Water	No.14	£0.25	......
Women Bishops?	No.15	£0.25	......
The Heavenly Vision	No.16	£0.25	......

Name and Address (in block capitals)

. . . .

. . . .

. . . .

If money is sent with order please allow for postage. Please address to:- The John Metcalfe Publishing Trust, Church Road, Tylers Green, Penn, Bucks, HP10 8LN.

Tract Order Form

Please send to the address below:-

    Price Quantity

Ecclesia Tracts

The Beginning of the Ecclesia	No.1	£0.10	......
Churches and the Church (J.N.D.)	No.2	£0.10	......
The Ministers of Christ	No.3	£0.10	......
The Inward Witness (G.F.)	No.4	£0.10	......
The Notion of a Clergyman (J.N.D.)	No.5	£0.10	......
The Servant of the Lord (W.H.)	No.6	£0.10	......
One Spirit (W.K.)	No.7	£0.10	......
The Funeral of Arminianism (W.H.)	No.8	£0.10	......
One Body (W.K.)	No.9	£0.10	......
False Churches and True	No.10	£0.10	......
Separation from Evil (J.N.D.)	No.11	£0.10	......
The Remnant (J.B.S.)	No.12	£0.10	......
The Arminian Skeleton (W.H.)	No.13	£0.10	......

Foundation Tracts

Female Priests?	No.1	£0.25	......
The Bondage of the Will (Martin Luther)	No.2	£0.25	......
Of the Popish Mass (John Calvin)	No.3	£0.25	......
The Adversary	No.4	£0.25	......
The Advance of Popery (J.C. Philpot)	No.5	£0.25	......
Enemies in the Land	No.6	£0.25	......
An Admonition Concerning Relics (John Calvin)	No.7	£0.25	......
John Metcalfe's Testimony against Falsity in Worship	No.8	£0.25	......

Name and Address (in block capitals)

. . . .

. . . .

. . . .

If money is sent with order please allow for postage. Please address to:- The John Metcalfe Publishing Trust, Church Road, Tylers Green, Penn, Bucks, HP10 8LN.